In this book, we're going to talk all about Labrador Retrievers. So, let's get right to it!

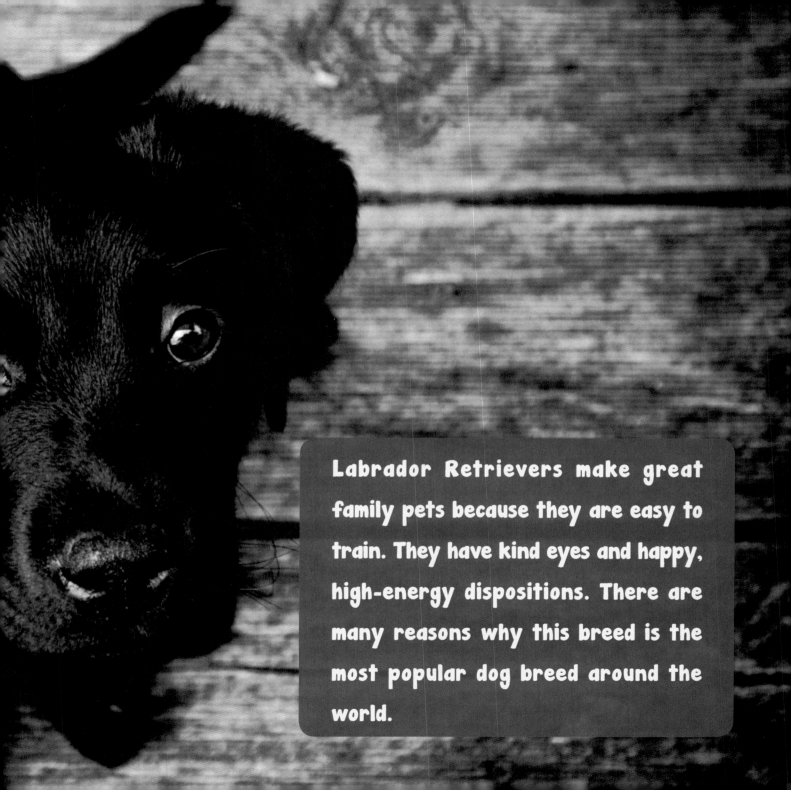

Labrador Retrievers make great family pets because they are easy to train. They have kind eyes and happy, high-energy dispositions. There are many reasons why this breed is the most popular dog breed around the world.

WHAT CAN YOU EXPECT
FROM YOUR LAB?

Labrador Retrievers are sometimes called Labradors or just Labs for short. Labs absolutely love being part of a family. They are very energetic and want to be taken out for walks, especially when they're puppies. They are a perfect choice for a high-energy family that wants a dog to be a vital part of their daily lives.

You should plan on going for plenty of walks with your Lab and you'll also spend a lot of time training your new pet. Labs are very affectionate and they're not territorial, so they don't make good guard dogs since they're naturally friendly, even to strangers!

Labs are hardy dogs, but they also have huge appetites so you have to control what they eat otherwise they can get obese. Weight problems and other health issues can give them hip dysplasia, which essentially means that their hips become disjointed.

Often used as companion dogs for handicapped people or sniffer dogs to help find illegal drugs, Labrador Retrievers are very easy to train.

HISTORY OF THE
LABRADOR RETRIEVER

Labrador Retrievers originally came from Newfoundland. They were working dogs that assisted fishermen as they brought in their catches from the cold waters surrounding Canada. Their coats were short and didn't get much ice in them, which was an advantage, but their coats were also dense and provided plenty of insulation.

Their semi-webbed feet and broad tails made them efficient swimmers. Later in their history, they were brought to the United Kingdom where they were bred to retrieve water birds during hunting expeditions.

Because of their amazing sense of smell, which is thousands of times more sensitive than human smelling, Labs have been trained to become sniffer dogs. For example, in Australia they have been trained to sniff out drugs as well as ammunition, chemicals, and explosives. Their excellent sense of smell, as well as their willingness to learn and to please their trainers, have made Labs exceptionally proficient as sniffer dogs.

Another area where they excel is by providing companionship for or becoming guide dogs for people who aren't mobile or have a handicap such as blindness. They can help by picking up items that are dropped or by alerting someone if their human companion is in trouble. They have even been taught to unload washing machines and pick up the phone. When they are walking with their handicapped human companions outdoors, they can press the pedestrian button so they can cross the street together.

ADVANTAGES AND DISADVANTAGES OF LABS

A Labrador Retriever might be the right pet for you if you're looking for a dog with these characteristics:

* Is large, excitable, filled with energy, and has bouncy enthusiasm about everything

* Has a short, dense coat that's easy to care for

* Has a happy disposition and is always wagging its tail

* Loves to exercise and play athletic games

* Is pretty calm, trustworthy, and dependable

* Is friendly toward other pets

* Is very responsive during training sessions and wants to please

In order to take care of a Lab responsibly you'll need to:

* Provide lots of exercise and stimulating activities every day

* Put up with jumping and some rowdiness when your Lab is a puppy or hasn't exercised enough

* Put up with "mouthiness," which simply means that Labs love to carry and chew things and might even mouth your hands when you're playing-remember, they were bred to pick up hunted birds

* Put up with lots of shedding all around the house
* Provide a large space for your pet to live in - Labs don't fit well in tiny, cramped apartments
* Give your pet plenty of attention and if you're not around make sure he or she has another dog to play with
* Make sure you can spend the money to feed your dog and protect him or her from parasites - because Labs are large, feeding them and keeping them healthy costs more than it does with smaller dogs

PHYSICAL CHARACTERISTICS OF LABS

When you're selecting your Labrador Retriever pet, you can choose one with either a yellow, black, or chocolate coat. The chocolate color is rare compared to the others. They do come in varying shades, but they're always in one of those three categories.

Labs are large dogs. Females generally weigh from 45 to 70 pounds and males generally weigh from 60 to 80 pounds. Most people think they have kind-looking eyes. Their coats are very smooth, short, and water resistant. They have a height of 22-24 inches from the ground to their withers, which are their shoulder blades.

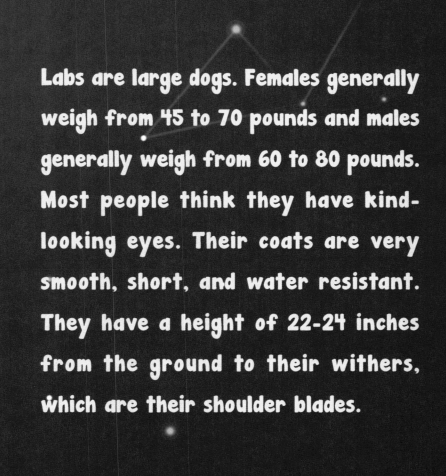

If they are well cared for, Labs live an average of 10-12 years.

EXERCISE AND TRAINING FOR YOUR LABRADOR RETRIEVER

Labs have a need for one to two hours daily of exercise and one to two hours daily for training. When they are puppies, they need at least two hours a day for each activity, so you have to be prepared to spend a lot of time. They have a great deal of vitality so if it isn't channeled properly into positive sessions of exercise and training, they can get bored or worse yet, destructive.

If they don't get the proper amount of exercise, they can easily get obese, which is dangerous for their health. They love their families, are very social, and want to participate in daily walks and games.

To Labs, training is a game and they will do anything to please their trainer and to get their treats. They are very intelligent and have been trained for complex work as sniffer dogs as well as companion dogs.

Labs enjoy swimming as well as chasing and retrieving things. They are well suited to these activities because of their background as working dogs for fishermen and hunters. They like being around other dogs, so park play dates are a good idea.

They don't do well if they are alone for long periods of time. For people who don't have much leisure time, they might not be the best pet choice, unless they have a big space and other dogs to play with.

As long as they have playtime outdoors for a few hours each day, they don't mind being indoors as long as there's enough room to roam around. They like being around their human family, both adults and kids. They wouldn't deliberately hurt a baby or toddler, but because they're quite large, they should be supervised until children get older. They usually do just fine with other pets, even cats or exotic pets, as long as they are supervised while they get used to them.

GROOMING PRACTICES FOR YOUR LABRADOR RETRIEVER

The bad news about Labs is that their hair goes everywhere. The good news is that their coats are short and dry easily so it's simple to groom them. Brushing your pet's coat every day and making sure he or she has a protein-rich and oil-rich diet can ensure good skin health and reduce the amount of shedding. Other than that issue, they are pretty easy to keep well-groomed.

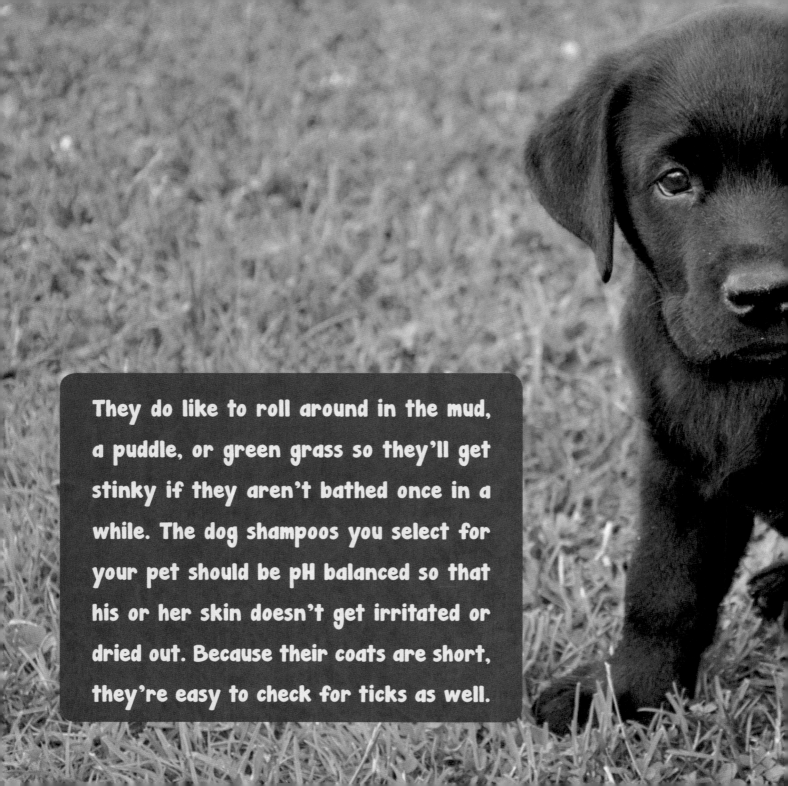

They do like to roll around in the mud, a puddle, or green grass so they'll get stinky if they aren't bathed once in a while. The dog shampoos you select for your pet should be pH balanced so that his or her skin doesn't get irritated or dried out. Because their coats are short, they're easy to check for ticks as well.

KEEPING YOUR LABRADOR RETRIEVER HEALTHY

There are three major things you can watch for to keep your Lab healthy.

MANAGE YOUR PET'S WEIGHT

Labradors have enormous appetites and if they get too fat it can cause health problems, such as the disease called cruciate ligament rupture. Consult with your vet to make sure you're feeding your Lab the proper amount of food daily. Overfeeding a growing puppy can cause lots of health problems as well, such as hip or elbow dysplasia.

TAKE CARE OF YOUR PET'S EARS

Because Labs have rather short ears, they are susceptible to ear infections. If you clean your pet's ears regularly, it can help to prevent ear troubles.

WATCH YOUR PET OUTDOORS

If you don't supervise your pet, he or she might eat things that shouldn't be consumed.

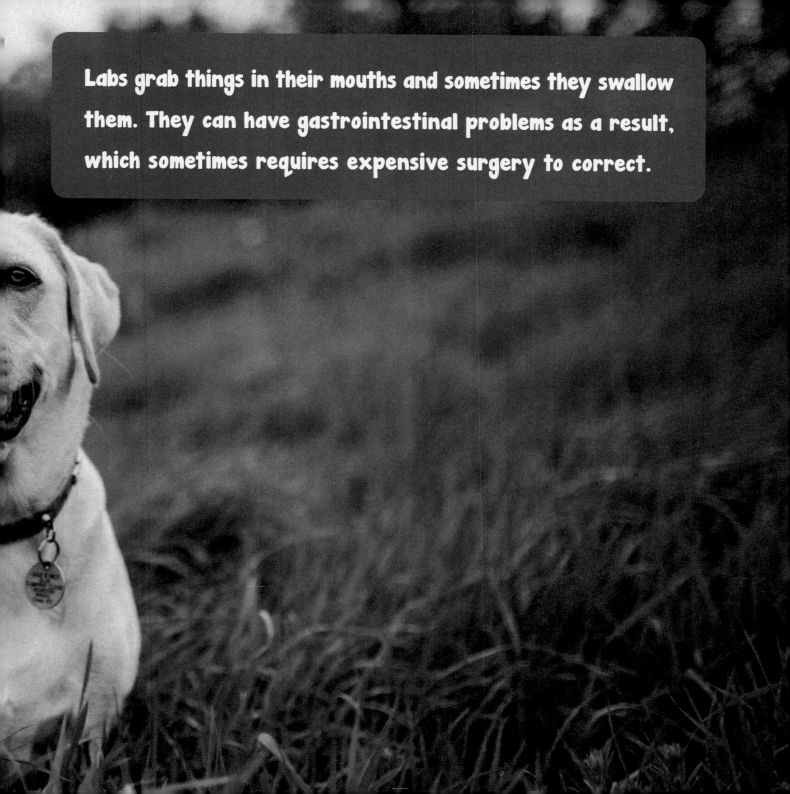

Labs grab things in their mouths and sometimes they swallow them. They can have gastrointestinal problems as a result, which sometimes requires expensive surgery to correct.

LABRADOR RETRIEVERS ARE VERY HELPFUL COMPANIONS

Labrador Retrievers are the most popular dog worldwide. They are big, lovable, affectionate and have a lot of energy. They make great family pets since they love both adults and kids. They're also very intelligent and can be trained as working companions, both as sniffer dogs and guide dogs for the handicapped.

Awesome! Now that you've read about Labrador Retrievers you may want to read about having a pony for a pet in the Pets Unchained book My Pony Loves To Gallop! | Horses Book for Children | Children's Horse Books.

Made in the USA
Monee, IL
30 November 2020

HEY THERE BUDDY!
LABRADOR RETRIEVER
KIDS BOOKS

Children's Dog Books

petsunchained
(PETS & ANIMALS)

Speedy Publishing LLC

40 E. Main St. #1156

Newark, DE 19711

www.speedypublishing.com

Copyright 2017